BRICK OF

DAD PUNS

Brick of Dad Puns:
Over 375 Pun-ishingly Hilarious Jokes

13-Digit ISBN: 978-1-64643-352-0
10-Digit ISBN: 1-64643-352-1

This book may be ordered by mail from the publisher. Please include $5.99 for postage and handling. Please support your local bookseller first!

Books published by Cider Mill Press Book Publishers are available at special discounts for bulk purchases in the United States by corporations, institutions, and other organizations. For more information, please contact the publisher.

Cider Mill Press Book Publishers
"Where good books are ready for press"
501 Nelson Place
Nashville, Tennessee 37214

cidermillpress.com

Typography: Adobe Garamond, BodoniFB, Clarendon, Futura, Hanley Sans, Helvetica, Industry Inc.

Printed in Malaysia

23 24 25 26 27 TJM 6 5 4 3 2

BRICK OF

DAD

PUNS

OVER 375
PUN–ISHINGLY
HILARIOUS
JOKES

CIDER MILL
PRESS

BOOK
PUBLISHERS

CONTENTS

INTRODUCTION

The dad joke has taken the world by storm, turning long car rides and trips to the hardware store into a nonstop wave of grumbling and eye-rolling while the teller of the joke smirks to themself. If you've been the unsuspecting victim of a dad joke, you've probably thought to yourself: "What could be worse than this?" Here in your hands you have a collection of something much, much worse than the average dad jokes: dad puns.

Dad puns take the delicious awkwardness of the dad joke and ramp it up into groan-worthy embarrassment. Dad puns use the most normal words and phrases to lure victims into a false sense of security before they deal the final pun-ishment.

Puns are the most intelligent and vicious jokes in a dad's repertoire, and these puns are guaranteed to earn you a death glare from the poor sucker standing in front of you. With enough practice in your bathroom mirror, you too can lovingly torture neighbors, friends, children, and unwitting café workers. And if anyone criticizes your punny jokes, you can politely remind them that Shakespeare loved puns, and therefore you are as funny and clever as the Bard himself.

If you find joy in telling jokes that cause passersby to cringe so hard that they may never be able to hear a joke again, then these cheesy-but-grate puns are perfect to keep in your arsenal of embarrassingly brilliant jokes that will make any barbecue or family dinner more enjoyable (for you, anyway).

CHAPTER 1

DID YOU HEAR...

Did you hear about the theater show about puns?

It was a play on words.

Did you hear about the band Duvet?

IT'S A COVER BAND.

Did you hear the joke about the peach?

It's pit-iful.

DID YOU HEAR ABOUT THE PRISON LIBRARY?

IT HAS ITS PROSE AND CONS.

Did you hear the balloon joke?

It's a bit long-winded.

Did you hear the garbage joke?

Actually, it's rubbish.

Did you hear about the child who skips rope and reads at the same time?

SHE ALWAYS JUMPS TO CONCLUSIONS.

Did you hear about the guy who invented the knock-knock joke?

HE WON THE NO-BELL PRIZE.

. . . .

Did you hear about the butter rumor?

YOU PROBABLY SHOULDN'T SPREAD IT.

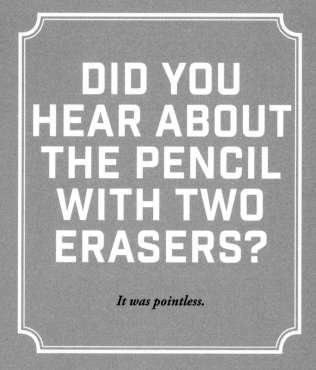

DID YOU HEAR ABOUT THE PENCIL WITH TWO ERASERS?

It was pointless.

Did you hear about the man who sued the airline for misplacing his luggage?

HE LOST HIS CASE.

· ·

Did you hear about the rowboat sale?

IT'S AN OAR-DEAL.

DID YOU HEAR ABOUT THE CHILD WHO WOULDN'T TAKE A NAP?

HE WAS RESISTING A REST.

DID YOU HEAR ABOUT THE TREE WHEN SPRING CAME?

It was re-leaved.

....

DID YOU HEAR ABOUT THE JOKE THAT WAS ALWAYS ON TIME?

It was very pun-ctual.

Did you hear about the really bad electrician?

PEOPLE WERE SHOCKED WHEN THEY FOUND OUT.

Did you hear about the kids who dressed up as almonds for Halloween?

EVERYONE THOUGHT THEY WERE NUTS.

DID YOU HEAR ABOUT THE KIDNAPPING AT SCHOOL?

DON'T WORRY, HE WOKE UP.

Did you hear about the percussionist running for office?

He's working on drumming up support.

Did you hear Peter Pan was kicked out of flight school?

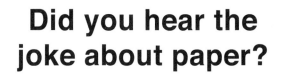

HE COULD NEVER LAND.

Did you hear the joke about paper?

IT'S TEAR-ABLE.

Did you hear about the two shepherds who became best friends even though they had

MUTTON IN COMMON?

DID YOU HEAR THE JOKE ABOUT THE BAD POLE VAULTER?

It never goes over very well.

....

DID YOU HEAR ABOUT THE SILENT BOWLING ALLEY?

It was so quiet you could hear a pin drop.

Did you hear about the fake hair that was really upset?

It really wigged out.

Did you hear about the sweaters that did everything together?

They were a close-knit group.

Did you hear about the short fortune-teller who escaped from jail?

It was a small medium at large.

DID YOU HEAR ABOUT THE RESTAURANT ON THE MOON?

GREAT FOOD, BUT NO ATMOSPHERE.

DID YOU HEAR THE OWL'S NEW JOKE?

IT WAS A HOOT.

Did you hear about the funny sea monster?

He's Kraken me up.

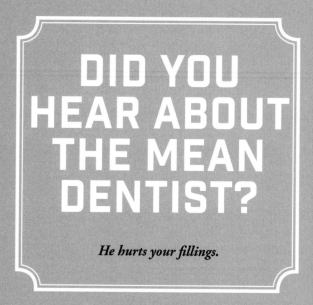

DID YOU HEAR ABOUT THE MEAN DENTIST?

He hurts your fillings.

Did you hear the joke about the omelette?

It was eggcellent.

Did you hear about the house that was painted white?

It paled in comparison to the previous color.

DID YOU HEAR THE PIG JOKE?

IT WAS BOAR-ING.

CHAPTER 2

WHAT DO YOU CALL...

WHAT DO YOU CALL A COW WITHOUT LEGS?

Ground beef.

. . . .

WHAT DO YOU CALL A PIG WHO DOES KARATE?

Pork chop.

WHAT DO YOU CALL A PLACE WHERE THEY MAKE THINGS THAT ARE JUST OKAY?

A SATISFACTORY.

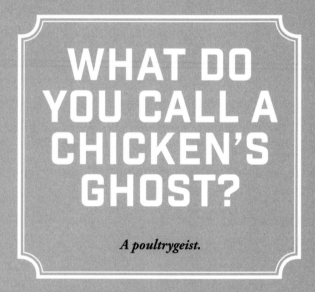

WHAT DO YOU CALL A CHICKEN'S GHOST?

A poultrygeist.

What do you call a pen without a top?

DE-CAP-ITATED.

What do you call a horse who disagrees with you?

A NEIGH-SAYER.

WHAT DO YOU CALL A BAGEL THAT CAN FLY?

A plane bagel.

....

WHAT DO YOU CALL A FAMOUS OCEAN ANIMAL?

A star-fish.

What do you call a rose talking on the phone?

A call-i-flower.

What do you call a haunted clothing shop?

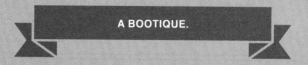

A BOOTIQUE.

What do you call a quick sketch of a New York baseball player?

A YANKEE DOODLE.

WHAT DO YOU CALL AN ANGRY PERSON WHO COMPETES IN A MARATHON?

A VERY CROSS COUNTRY RUNNER.

What do you call a couple of keets?

Parakeets.

WHAT DO YOU CALL A VET WITH LARYNGITIS?

A hoarse doctor.

....

WHAT DO YOU CALL A CONCEITED VAMPIRE?

A vein monster.

What do you call a skeleton that refuses to work?

LAZY BONES.

What do you call a priest that becomes a lawyer?

A father in law.

What do you call a book about blankets?

A cover story.

WHAT DO YOU CALL A VERY YOUNG CANNON?

A BABY BOOMER.

What do you call a coffee cup with no sense of fashion?

ONE UGLY MUG.

What do you call a chef that's on strike?

A COOKOUT.

WHAT DO YOU CALL TOO MANY ALIENS?

EXTRATERRESTRIALS.

What do you call a broken can opener?

A CAN'T OPENER.

What do you call the change in your pockets that goes through the washing machine?

Laundered money.

What do you call an alligator with a GPS?

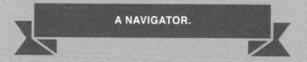

A NAVIGATOR.

What do you call two octopuses that look exactly the same?

ITENTACLE.

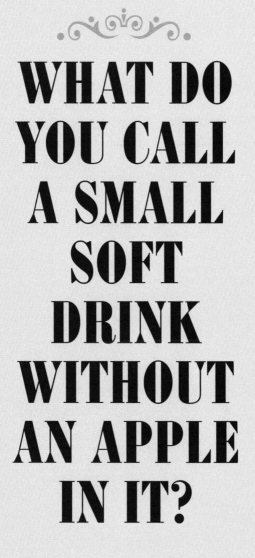

WHAT DO YOU CALL A SMALL SOFT DRINK WITHOUT AN APPLE IN IT?

A MINI APPLE-LESS MINI SODA.

WHAT DO YOU CALL COWBOY CLOTHES?

Ranch dressing.

....

WHAT DO YOU CALL A PEA THAT FALLS OFF THE PLATE?

An escapee.

What do you call a knight who's too scared to joust?

SIR RENDER.

What do you call an invisible golf course?

THE MISSING LINKS.

What do you call a photograph of a baseball thrower hanging on the wall?

A pitcher framed.

What do you call two siblings who take your money?

Fine brothers.

WHAT DO YOU CALL AN EXACT DUPLICATE OF TEXAS?

The Clone Star State.

WHAT DO YOU CALL AN OLD PIECE OF INSECT FURNITURE?

AN ANT-IQUE.

CHAPTER 3

WHY...

WHY WAS THE COUPLE'S CAMPSITE ALWAYS STRESSED?

Everything was two in tents.

....

WHY ARE RICH ENGLISHMEN SO STRONG?

All their money is measured in pounds.

Why did the playing card become a ship?

IT WANTED TO BE A FULL DECK.

Why was the sink so tired?

IT WAS FEELING DRAINED.

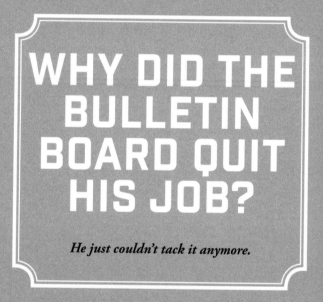

WHY DID THE BULLETIN BOARD QUIT HIS JOB?

He just couldn't tack it anymore.

Why did the wheel get an education?

Because it wanted to be well rounded.

WHY DID THE CHEF PUT A CLOCK IN A HOT PAN?

HE WANTED TO SEE TIME FRY.

Why did the family sell their vacuum?

It was just collecting dust.

Why did the referee get a new phone?

BECAUSE HE KEPT MISSING CALLS.

Why did the man accidentally call the hole in the ground a sewer?

HE MEANT WELL.

WHY WAS THE PHILOSOPHER SO BUSY?

Because he had a lot on his Plato.

....

WHY DID REARRANGING THE FURNITURE HELP THE RESTAURANT?

Because now the tables have turned.

Why do the numbers 1 to 12 work the hardest?

They're on the clock.

Why do cakes smell so good?

THEY HAVE A LOT OF FLOWER.

Why did the cookie go to the doctor?

BECAUSE HE WAS FEELING CRUMMY.

WHY DID THE BANANA GO TO THE DOCTOR?

BECAUSE HE WASN'T PEELING WELL.

WHY WON'T TEDDY BEARS EAT DESSERT?

THEY'RE ALWAYS STUFFED.

Why did the newlyweds buy stale baguettes?

They wanted to grow mold together.

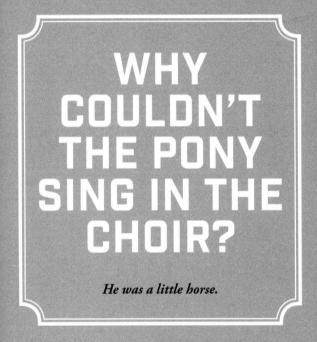

WHY COULDN'T THE PONY SING IN THE CHOIR?

He was a little horse.

Why are pastries so stupid?

THEY DONUT KNOW ANYTHING.

WHY ARE SKELETONS SO LONELY?

They have no body.

....

WHY ARE RUSSIAN DOLLS SO CONCEITED?

Because they're full of themselves.

Why was the ocean being investigated?

Because it was a bit fishy.

Why did the shoe go to heaven?

IT HAD A GOOD SOLE.

Why are concert halls so cold?

BECAUSE THEY'RE USUALLY FULL OF FANS.

WHY DID THE MAN GET FIRED FROM THE CALENDAR FACTORY?

HE TOOK A COUPLE DAYS OFF.

Why couldn't the photographer take a picture of the fog?

He mist his chance.

WHY DO EGGS LOVE THESE PUNS?

They crack them up.

. . . .

WHY SHOULDN'T YOU BELIEVE AN ATOM?

Because they make up everything.

WHY SHOULD YOU ALWAYS WASH A CHEESE SLICER AFTER USING IT?

FOR THE GRATER GOOD.

Why should you never whisper secrets on a farm?

Because the corn has ears.

Why wasn't the cat a good storyteller?

BECAUSE IT HAD ONE TAIL.

Why can't the ocean lie very well?

Because people can sea right through it.

WHY DID THE LAWYER HAVE MEXICAN FOOD FOR LUNCH?

TO GET SOME CASE-IDEAS.

WHY WAS THE NORSE GOD BANNED FROM PLAYING GAMES?

HE WAS A THOR LOSER.

Why was the woman fired from the candle factory?

SHE WOULDN'T WORK WICK-ENDS.

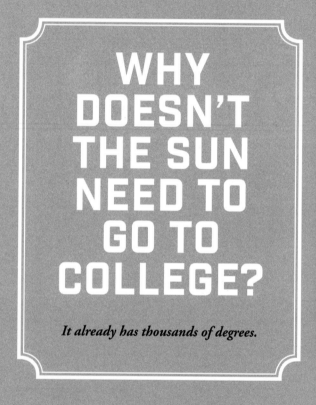

WHY DOESN'T THE SUN NEED TO GO TO COLLEGE?

It already has thousands of degrees.

Why did the gym close down?

It wasn't working out.

Why can't towels tell good jokes?

BECAUSE THEY HAVE
A DRY SENSE OF HUMOR.

Why did the sick shoe go to the cobbler?

IT WANTED TO BE HEELED.

Why do doctors make good parents?

They have plenty of patients.

WHY ARE EVERYBODY'S PANTS TOO SHORT?

THEIR LEGS ALWAYS STICK OUT TWO FEE

WHY DO CHAMELEONS MAKE GREAT PARTY GUESTS?

They always blend in.

....

WHY WAS THE LION SAD AND LONELY?

He had no pride.

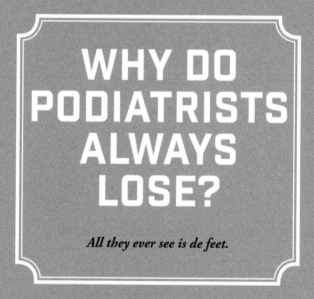

WHY DO PODIATRISTS ALWAYS LOSE?

All they ever see is de feet.

Why was the old house crying?

It had windowpanes.

Why shouldn't you gamble in the jungle?

THERE'S TOO MANY CHEETAHS.

Why don't trees exercise?

WORKING OUT SAPS THEIR STRENGTH.

Why did the skeleton refuse to go on the rollercoaster?

He didn't have the guts.

WHY DID THE THERMOMETER GO TO COLLEGE?

IT WANTED A HIGHER DEGREE.

WHY DOES THE PRESIDENT COVER HIS EYES WHEN HE WALKS THROUGH HIS KITCHEN?

HE WANTS TO AVOID ANOTHER CABINET MEETING.

Why can't you find any brooms in New York?

IT'S THE CITY THAT NEVER SWEEPS.

Why is a school like a kingdom?

THEY BOTH HAVE LOTS OF SUBJECTS.

Why was the inchworm angry?

HE HAD TO CONVERT
TO THE METRIC SYSTEM.

Why was Frankenstein walking funny?

HE HAD A MONSTER WEDGIE.

Why did the monster go to the monster go to the hospital?

To have his
ghoulstones removed.

Why didn't the mummy take a vacation?

He was wrapped up in his work.

Why are skeletons bad baseball players?

THEY MAKE TOO MANY
BONEHEADED PLAYS.

Why do witches wear name tags at the spell-casting convention?

SO THEY KNOW WHICH WITCH IS WHICH.

Why did the tennis fan go to an eye doctor?

BECAUSE EVERY TIME HE WATCHED A MATCH HE SAW DOUBLES.

WHY DID THE CATERPILLAR GO OUT FOR THE SWIM TEAM?

He wanted to learn the butterfly stroke.

....

WHY IS A TENNIS COURT SO NOISY?

Because tennis players always raise a racket.

WHY ARE COMEDIANS NOT ALLOWED TO ICE-SKATE?

THEY MAKE THE ICE CRACK UP.

Why was the arrow so angry?

It was fired from a crossbow.

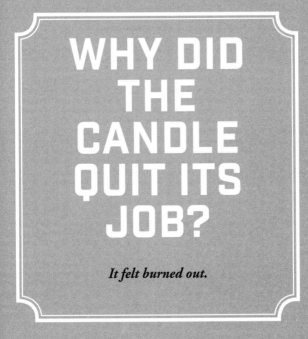

WHY DID THE CANDLE QUIT ITS JOB?

It felt burned out.

Why did the broken chair lose an argument?

It didn't have a leg to stand on.

WHY WAS THE PIANO GIGGLING?

Someone was tickling its keys.

. . . .

WHY IS AN EDITOR'S DESK ALWAYS COLD?

There are too many drafts.

Why are showers always in trouble?

THEY'RE ALWAYS IN HOT WATER.

Why was money falling from the sky?

THERE WAS A CHANGE IN THE WEATHER.

WHY DID THE DONUT SHOP CLOSE?

THE OWNER WAS TIRED OF THE HOLE BUSINESS.

WHY DID THE PLUM ASK THE CHERRY TO DINNER?

It couldn't find a date.

. . . .

WHY DID THE EGG COMEDIAN FAIL?

All it had was bad yolks.

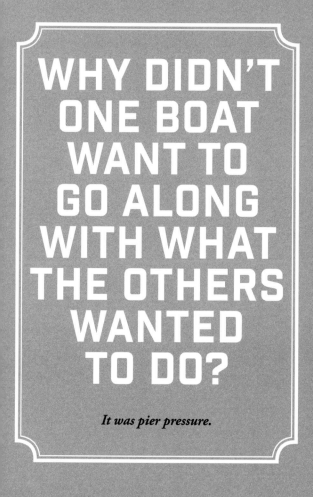

WHY DIDN'T ONE BOAT WANT TO GO ALONG WITH WHAT THE OTHERS WANTED TO DO?

It was pier pressure.

WHY DID THE WOMAN USING AN UMBRELLA LOOK SICK?

BECAUSE SHE WAS UNDER THE WEATHER.

Why are houses with basements more popular?

Because they're best cellars.

Why couldn't the ventriloquist do last night's show?

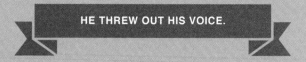

HE THREW OUT HIS VOICE.

....

Why can't lamps be trusted?

THEY'RE TOO SHADY.

WHY ARE FISH GREAT AT DOING MATH?

THEY MULTIPLY FAST.

WHY DID THE TEACHER BRING BIRDSEED TO SCHOOL?

She had a parrot-teacher conference after class.

....

WHY DID THE WOMAN DIVORCE THE HISTORY TEACHER?

He insisted on living in the past.

Why was the dog named Rolex?

HE WAS A WATCHDOG.

Why did the banker quit his job?

HE LOST INTEREST.

Why are circles so useless?

BECAUSE THEY'RE POINTLESS.

Why did the tree want more friends?

IT WANTED TO BRANCH OUT.

Why did the woman run around her bed?

TO CATCH UP ON HER SLEEP.

WHY WAS THE HALF MAN, HALF HORSE ALWAYS BRAGGING?

HE HAD TO BE THE
CENTAUR OF ATTENTION.

Why couldn't the walnut shell get a job?

Because it was a nut case.

WHY DID THE ACTOR END UP IN THE HOSPITAL?

**EVERYONE TOLD HIM
TO BREAK A LEG.**

Why did the miner go to the podiatrist?

He had coal feet.

WHY DID THE EAGLE GO TO THE DOCTOR?

He had a soar throat.

WHY DID THE WINDOW SHADE GO TO THE PSYCHOLOGIST?

IT WAS UP-TIGHT.

Why did the baby rocket go to the doctor?

It was time for his booster.

Why did Frankenstein's monster go to the ER?

HE WAS IN SHOCK.

Why did the turtles take their son to the psychologist?

THEY COULDN'T GET HIM TO COME OUT OF HIS SHELL.

WHY DO PRISON WARDENS CARRY FACE WASH?

It helps them prevent breakouts.

....

WHY DID THE BASEBALL PLAYER STAY INSIDE?

He was afraid of getting out.

Why do basketball players spend so much time at home?

Because they're not allowed to travel.

Why are fishermen great singers?

THEY KNOW A TUNA TWO.

Why does the boxer never silence his phone?

HE LIKES THE RING.

Why didn't the Olympic diver run for political office?

HE HAD NO PLATFORM.

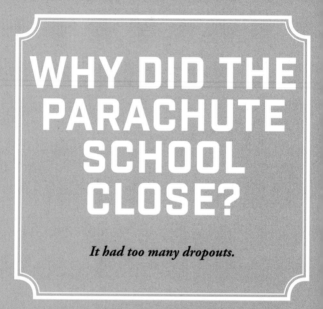

WHY DID THE PARACHUTE SCHOOL CLOSE?

It had too many dropouts.

Why are kittens bad at jokes?

They take everything litterally.

WHY DID THE TIGHTROPE WALKER QUIT THE CIRCUS?

HE FINALLY REACHED THE END OF HIS ROPE.

Why did the poker player run to the bathroom?

He had a flush.

CHAPTER 4

PERSONAL ANECDOTES

I used to be a hockey player.

I GOT SICK OF JUST SKATING BY.

I used to make stencils for a living.

I HAD MY WORK CUT OUT FOR ME.

I used to want to be a paleontologist.

BUT I REALIZED IT WAS A MAMMOTH MISTAKE.

I USED TO
MAKE BEER,

but everyone was always so brewed.

. . . .

I USED TO BE
AN ARTIST,

but I couldn't palette that life anymore.

I used to work at an origami store,

BUT THEN THE BUSINESS FOLDED.

I used to be a mason,

BUT PEOPLE KEPT TAKING ME FOR GRANITE.

I used to be a clockmaker,

BUT IT REALLY STARTED TO TICK ME OFF.

I used to be a baker,

BUT THAT GOT STALE FAST.

I used to make jokes about the Civil War.

GENERAL LEE, THEY WEREN'T THAT FUNNY.

I used to be obsessed with vegetables.

Now I don't carrot all.

I used to work as a cheese taster.

But I didn't think it was a gouda-nough career for me.

I USED TO TELL A LOT OF SCIENCE JOKES.

NOW ALL THE GOOD
ONES ARGON.

I used to be a personal trainer.

THEN I GAVE MY TOO WEAK NOTICE.

. . . .

I used to work at a feline café,

BUT EVERYONE WAS TOO CATTY.

I used to sail a ship full of violins for a living.

IT WAS A BOATLOAD OF TREBLE.

I used to study evolution.

IT WAS A NATURAL SELECTION, REALLY.

I used to work at a medieval fair.

It really plagues me to think about it.

I USED TO WORK IN OUTER SPACE.

THE PAY WAS OUT OF THIS WORLD.

I can cut wood just by looking at it.

IT'S TRUE—I SAW IT WITH MY OWN EYES.

MY WIFE REFUSES TO DO KARAOKE WITH ME.

I HAVE TO DUET ALONE.

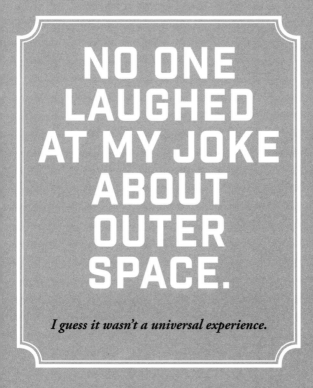

NO ONE LAUGHED AT MY JOKE ABOUT OUTER SPACE.

I guess it wasn't a universal experience.

Did you know that my friend broke her thumb yesterday?

ON THE OTHER HAND, SHE'S FINE.

MY SISTER BET I COULDN'T MAKE A CAR OUT OF SPAGHETTI.

YOU SHOULD HAVE SEEN HER FACE WHEN I DROVE PASTA.

My sister, my aunt, and my mother all have holes in their tights.

It runs in the family.

I MET AN ASTRONAUT, BUT WE HAVEN'T SEEN EACH OTHER SINCE.

I GUESS WE TRAVEL IN DIFFERENT ORBITS.

I've been telling everyone about the benefits of eating dried grapes.

I'M ALL ABOUT RAISIN AWARENESS.

I HATE JOKES ABOUT GERMAN SAUSAGES.

THEY'RE THE WURST.

CHAPTER 5

WHAT DID THEY SAY?

WHAT DID THE COFFEE SAY TO HIS DATE?

"You're brew-tiful."

....

WHAT DID ONE CEMETERY SAY TO THE OTHER?

"Are you plotting against me?"

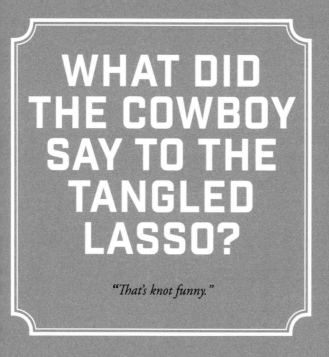

WHAT DID THE COWBOY SAY TO THE TANGLED LASSO?

"That's knot funny."

What did the fast car say to the sharp curve?

"It was an honor to swerve you."

What did the handyman say to the wall?

"ONE MORE CRACK LIKE THAT AND I'LL PLASTER YOU."

What did the price tag yell at the checkout counter?

"HELP! I'VE BEEN RIPPED OFF."

What did one cabinet say to the other?

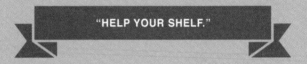

"HELP YOUR SHELF."

What did the chef say as the water boiled away?

"YOU WILL BE MIST."

WHAT DID THEY SAY TO THE GUY WHO INVENTED ZERO?

"Thanks for nothing."

....

WHAT DID THE FARMER SAY TO THE SHEEP THAT WAS HIDING?

"I see ewe!"

What did the arm bone say to the funny bone?

"You're very humerus."

What did the old lawn chair say to the new lawn chair?

"WELCOME TO THE FOLD."

....

What did one duck football player say to the other duck football player?

"LET'S PUDDLE UP."

What did the hockey coach say to the player who was caught breaking team rules?

"WATCH YOUR STEP! YOU'RE SKATING ON THIN ICE."

WHAT DID THE CLOTHESLINE SAY TO THE WET LAUNDRY?

"YOU'RE REALLY DAMPENING THE MOOD."

WHAT DID ONE SPEAKER SYSTEM SAY TO THE OTHER?

"I have some sound advice for you."

....

WHAT DID THE MEASLES SAY TO THE CHICKEN POX?

"Don't do anything rash."

What did the hog say after it lay in the hot sun too long?

"I'M BACON OUT HERE."

What did the clumsy person say after he spilled his soup?

"DON'T WORRY EVERYONE— LUNCH IS ON ME!"

What did the catcher's mitt say to the baseball?

"Catch you later!"

WHAT DID THE NOSE SAY TO THE INDEX FINGER?

"STOP PICKING ON ME."

What did the broken clock say?

"WILL SOMEONE GIVE ME A HAND?"

WHAT DID THE SHOVEL SAY TO THE HOLE?

"Let's get to the bottom of this."

....

WHAT DID THE BEACH SAY WHEN THE TIDE CAME IN?

"Long time, no sea."

What did the man who walked into a bar with a piece of concrete say?

"I'LL HAVE A DRINK, AND ONE FOR THE ROAD."

What did the dentist say on the woman's fourth visit?

"YOU KNOW THE DRILL."

What did the conductor say when he found his missing sheet music?

"SCORE!"

What did the pig marshal say to the hog outlaw?

"REACH FOR THE STY, PARDNER."

WHAT DID NICK SAY WHEN HIS FRIEND ASKED FOR FIVE CENTS?

"I'm Nicholas."

. . . .

WHAT DID ONE STREET RACER SAY TO THE OTHER?

"This job is getting to be a real drag."

WHAT DID THE CHILD SAY WHEN HIS MOTHER TOLD HIM NOT TO SWIM ON A FULL STOMACH?

"OKAY, MOM. I'LL SWIM BACKSTROKE."

WHAT DID THE MOM FIRE SAY TO THE DAD FIRE?

"I'M SO PROUD OF ARSON."

What did the calf say to the silo?

"IS MY FODDER IN THERE?"

....

What did the gas oven say to the furnace?

"YOU'VE REALLY GOT ME FUMING."

WHAT DID THE DRAPES SAY TO THE DECORATOR?

"DON'T SASH ME."

WHAT DID THE HOLE SAY TO THE TRENCH?

"Let's ditch your friend."

What did the lasso say to the steer that escaped?

"I guess you're not in the loop anymore."

What did the doctor say to the feather mattress before telling him bad news?

"You might want to lie down for this."

WHAT DID THE HAND SAY TO THE ARM?

"HOW ABOUT GIVING ME A RAISE?"

What did the dying window shout?

"IT'S CURTAINS FOR ME!"

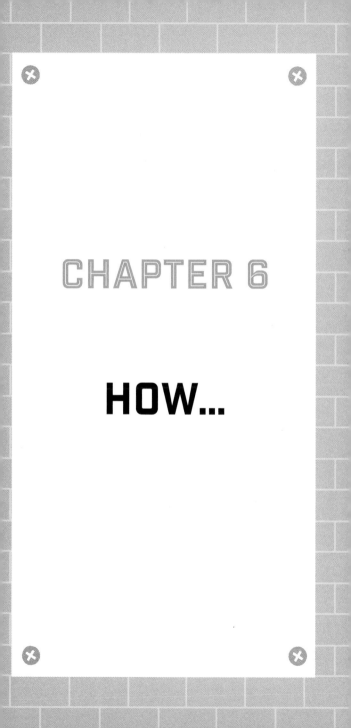

CHAPTER 6

HOW...

HOW DOES DARTH VADER KNOW WHAT LUKE GOT HIM FOR CHRISTMAS?

He felt his presents.

....

HOW DO YOU FIX A BROKEN TUBA?

With a tuba glue.

How do you catch a unique rabbit?

UNIQUE UP ON HIM.

How much does a pirate pay for corn?

A BUCCANEER.

How many tickles does it take to make an octopus laugh?

TEN-TICKLES.

How long does a jousting match last?

Until knight fall.

How does a Yeti build his house?

Igloos it together.

How does a train eat?

IT GOES CHEW CHEW.

....

How did the Egyptians select the next pharaoh?

IT WAS A PYRAMID SCHEME.

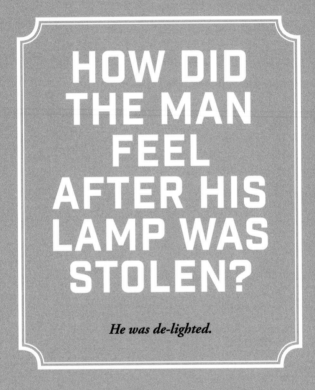

HOW DID THE MAN FEEL AFTER HIS LAMP WAS STOLEN?

He was de-lighted.

HOW DO SPIDERS COMMUNICATE?

THROUGH THE WORLD WIDE WEB.

How did the tree get online?

It logged in.

How do rabbits fly to Europe?

They take a hare plane.

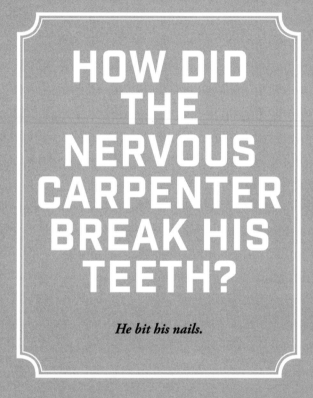

HOW DID THE NERVOUS CARPENTER BREAK HIS TEETH?

He bit his nails.

HOW DO OFFENSIVE LINEMEN CELEBRATE A VICTORY?

THEY THROW A BLOCK PARTY.

How do you lock up a motel?

Use a hotel chain.

HOW DO YOU CLEAN A DIRTY SPACE MONSTER?

Chase it through a meteor shower.

. . . .

HOW DO YOU UNLOCK A HAUNTED HOUSE?

Use a skeleton key.

HOW DO YOU BRIGHTEN UP A DULL GARDEN?

With a light bulb.

. . . .

HOW DO YOU DIAL A CELL PHONE?

Use your ring finger.

How did the bird learn to fly?

It just winged it.

HOW DOES A CON MAN SLEEP?

HE LIES ON ONE SIDE AND THEN LIES ON THE OTHER.

How much space should you plan to use for growing fungi?

AS MUSHROOM AS POSSIBLE.

How do you defend a castle made out of cheese?

WITH A MOAT-ZARELLA.

HOW DO YOU SAFELY HANDLE A BABY GOAT?

Use kid gloves.

....

HOW CAN YOU START A FIRE WITH A SEARCH ENGINE?

Ask, and you'll get a lot of matches.

How do spies keep warm?

THEY GO UNDERCOVER.

How do you fix a train that can't hear so well?

With an engine-ear.

How do you tell if someone has bucket fever?

THEY LOOK KIND OF PAIL.

. . . .

How do pool players play poker?

THEY USE CUE CARDS.

HOW DID THE PICTURE END UP IN JAIL?

IT WAS FRAMED.

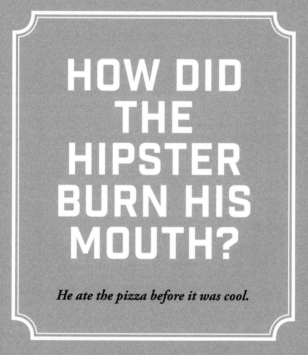

HOW DID THE HIPSTER BURN HIS MOUTH?

He ate the pizza before it was cool.

CHAPTER 7

WHAT...

What kind of drink can be hard to swallow?

REALI-TEA.

What happened to the house whose toilet was stolen?

POLICE HAD NOTHING TO GO ON.

WHAT DID THE TWO CATS DO AFTER ARGUING?

Hiss and make up.

....

WHAT KIND OF FISH HAS THE BIGGEST SHOES?

Clown fish.

What kind of candy bar is the funniest?

Snickers.

What kind of music does a mountain listen to?

Classic rock.

WHAT DID THE PIRATE BUY AFTER HE GOT HIS PATCH?

AN EYE-PHONE.

What kind of career did the boat want to go into?

SAILS.

. . . .

What does a tree wear with its shirt?

A PAIR OF PLANTS.

What type
of sandals
does a frog
wear?

Open-toad.

What's the most musical part of a fish?

THE SCALES.

WHAT KIND OF MUSIC DO MUMMIES LIKE?

Wrap.

What does a vegetarian zombie eat?

GRAINS.

What do you give a citrus fruit that needs help?

LEMON AID.

WHAT HAPPENS WHEN YOU TOSS SMALL OVENS INTO THE WATER?

You get microwaves.

....

WHAT'S THE BEST WAY TO KEEP YOUR BAGEL FROM BEING STOLEN?

Put some lox on it.

What happened when the students tied their shoes all together?

They took a class trip.

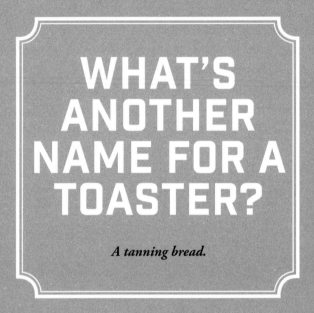

WHAT'S ANOTHER NAME FOR A TOASTER?

A tanning bread.

WHAT SIDE DISH DID THE RULERS OF RUSSIA LIKE THE MOST?

Tsardines.

....

WHAT DID THE YOUNG SAILOR GET ON HIS REPORT CARD?

Seven C's.

WHAT HAPPENED TO THE MAN WHO SWALLOWED SEVERAL SMALL PLASTIC HORSES?

THE DOCTOR SAID HIS CONDITION WAS STABLE.

WHAT HAPPENED TO THE MAN WHO WANTED A BRAIN TRANSPLANT?

HE CHANGED HIS MIND.

What kind of clothes do storm clouds wear?

THUNDERWEAR.

What happens if you bother someone while they're working on a puzzle?

YOU HEAR SOME CROSSWORDS.

What kind of boat does a dentist ride on?

A tooth ferry.

WHAT DOES A LIBRARIAN PLAY GOLF WITH?

A BOOK CLUB.

What do space squirrels like to eat?

ASTRONUTS.

What casts spells and plays croquet?

A WICKET WITCH.

WHAT IS A MERMAN'S FAVORITE SHIRT?

A WATER POLO.

What do union leaders and baseball umpires have in common?

They both have the power to call strikes.

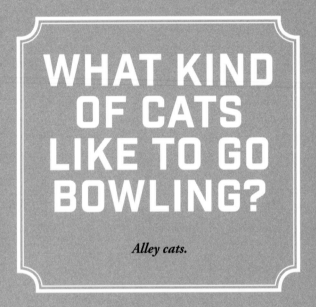

WHAT KIND OF CATS LIKE TO GO BOWLING?

Alley cats.

What happens when young cows do lots of leg lifts?

THEY GET GREAT CALF MUSCLES.

What do you get if you kiss glue?

LIP STICK.

What kind of bird insults people?

A MOCKINGBIRD.

What kind of book should you bring to music class?

A note pad.

WHAT KIND OF ESSAY DOES A TOUGH JUDGE WRITE?

ONE THAT HAS LOTS OF LONG SENTENCES.

What do dancers drink with their lunch?

TAP WATER.

What makes dinosaurs itch and scratch?

A fleahistoric bug.

What kind of horse does a cowboy ghost ride?

A night mare.

WHAT DID DRACULA GET WHEN HE BIT THE ABOMINABLE SNOWMAN?

Frost bite.

. . . .

WHAT DO WITCHES NEED ON THEIR COMPUTER?

Spell check.

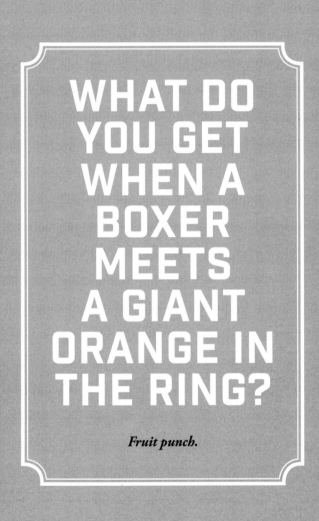

WHAT DO YOU GET WHEN A BOXER MEETS A GIANT ORANGE IN THE RING?

Fruit punch.

What are astronomers' favorite sports teams?

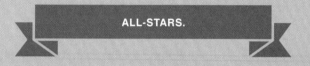

ALL-STARS.

- -

What do you hear when a cyclist is deep in thought?

HIS WHEELS TURNING.

WHAT DO YOU GET IF YOU CROSS A DIAPER AND A HANDBAG?

A CHANGE PURSE.

WHAT DID THE LITTLE PEBBLES GO DOWN AT THE PLAYGROUND?

The rock slide.

....

WHAT HAPPENS AFTER MUSICIANS DIE?

They de-compose.

WHAT'S THE DEFINITION OF A VACCINATION?

A JAB WELL DONE.

WHAT DO YOU GET FROM A COW THAT'S BEEN PAMPERED?

SPOILED MILK.

What happens if you don't pay the exorcist his fee?

You get repossessed.

What kind of climbing device marries into the family?

A STEP-LADDER.

What did the woman who was afraid of elevators do?

She took steps to avoid them.

WHAT ARE THE STRONGEST DAYS OF THE WEEK?

SATURDAY AND SUNDAY; THE REST ARE WEAK-DAYS.

What do cows tell their children at bedtime?

DAIRY TALES.

What is a soup's favorite sport?

BOWL-ING.

What do Wall Street cows invest in?

Mootual funds.

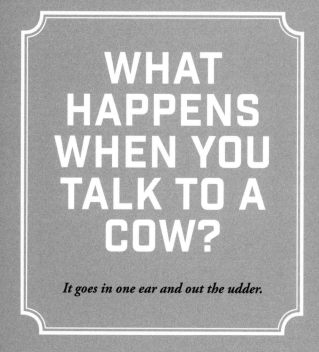

WHAT HAPPENS WHEN YOU TALK TO A COW?

It goes in one ear and out the udder.

What do you use to catch a school of fish?

Bookworms.

WHAT'S THE BEST MUSICAL INSTRUMENT?

WELL, ACCORDION TO A NEW SURVEY...

What happened when the rainbow took a test?

It passed with flying colors.

What do you get when a piano falls down a mine shaft?

A-FLAT MINER.

What do you do if you're Hungary?

CZECH THE MENU.

What will going to bed with music on give you?

A sound sleep.

WHAT'S THE PROBLEM WITH LONG FANTASY STORIES?

THEY TEND TO DRAGON.

What do baseball players eat on?

HOME PLATES.

What happens when you get a bladder infection?

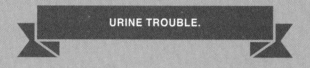

URINE TROUBLE.

....

What do you get if you cross a star and a podiatrist?

TWINKLE TOES.

WHAT DO YOU GET WHEN YOU DON'T REFRIGERATE AN ATHLETE?

A SPOILED SPORT.

What role did the hockey player play in *A Midsummer Night's Dream*?

Puck.

What happened when the sink and the bathtub started an advertising campaign?

THEY PLUGGED THEMSELVES.

WHAT DOES A NOVEL WEAR TO KEEP WARM?

A dust jacket.

....

WHAT KIND OF DOTS DANCE?

Polka dots.

What do you get if you cross a traffic light and a bonfire?

A smoke signal.

What will happen to you after telling all these jokes?

You'll get pun-ished.

CHAPTER 8

EVEN MORE PUNNY JOKES

Where can you find polluted belts?

Around toxic waists.

WHERE DID THE JUDGE PLAY ON THE COURT SOFTBALL TEAM?

NOWHERE. THE JUDGE WAS ON THE BENCH.

Where do phlebotomists go to college?

IV LEAGUE SCHOOLS.

Where does a bird borrow books?

AT THE FLYBRARY.

If the Marines can't do the job, who do you send in?

THE SUB-MARINES.

Where do you put a Christmas tree?

Between a Christmas two and a Christmas four.

DID YOU AT LEAST FINNISH YOUR FOOD?

YES, BUT THERE WAS NORWAY
I COULD EAT ANY MORE.

Do you think this glass coffin will be successful?

Remains to be seen.

Where do cows eat their lunch?

In a calf-eteria.

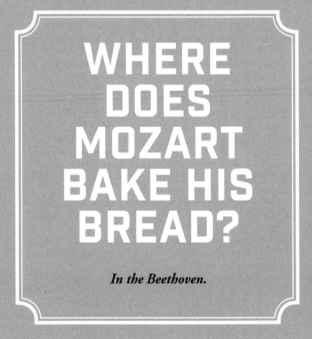

WHERE DOES MOZART BAKE HIS BREAD?

In the Beethoven.

WHERE CAN YOU IMPRISON A SKELETON?

IN A RIB CAGE.

If you learn enough of these jokes, what will you be?

PUN-STOPPABLE.

CAN
FEBRUARY
MARCH?

No, but April May.

. . . .

WHEN SHOULD
YOU WRAP A
TV SHOW IN A
BLANKET?

When it has a cold open.

When is a bloodhound dumb?

WHEN HE HAS NO SCENTS.

Where do clams go to work out?

MUSSEL BEACH.

WHICH DOCTOR HAS THE BEST VOICE?

THE CHOIRPRACTOR.

Where did the Tin Man go after he retired?

A rust home.

Where do automobiles go to have fun?

THE CAR-NIVAL.

DO YOU KNOW THE WOMAN FROM THE VEGETARIAN CLUB?

NO, I'VE NEVER MET HERBIVORE.

DO YOU LIKE USING STRAWS?

No, those are for suckers.

Have you been to the funny mountain?

It's hill-arious.

Which of King Arthur's knights was shaped like a circle?

Sir Cumference.

DID YOU READ THE NEW BOOK ABOUT ANTI-GRAVITY?

IT'S IMPOSSIBLE TO PUT DOWN.

Where do ravens like to drink?

At the crowbar.

If we breathe oxygen in the day, what do we breathe at night?

Night-trogen.

When is a door not a door?

WHEN IT'S AJAR.

How do you organize a space party?

YOU PLANET.

When does a duck wake up?

At the quack of dawn.

WHICH STATE IS VERY COLD IN THE WINTER?

BURRMONT.

Which state is the trouser state?

Pantsylvania.

WANT TO HEAR A JOKE ABOUT A HAMSTER?

IT REALLY GETS YOUR WHEELS SPINNING.

When does a joke become a dad joke?

WHEN IT'S FULLY GROAN.

ABOUT CIDER MILL PRESS BOOK PUBLISHERS

Good ideas ripen with time. From seed to harvest, Cider Mill Press strives to bring fine reading, information, and entertainment together between the covers of its creatively crafted books. Our Cider Mill bears fruit twice a year, publishing a new crop of titles each spring and fall.

501 Nelson Place
Nashville, Tennessee 37214

cidermillpress.com